UNDERSTANDING LEARNING
the How, the Why, the What

Payne, Ruby K., Ph.D.
 Understanding Learning: the How, the Why, the What
Copyright © 2002, **aha!** Process, Inc. 91 pp.
  Bibliography pp. 83-91
  ISBN 1-929229-04-6

Other selected titles by Ruby K. Payne, Ph.D.

A Framework for Understanding Poverty
*Un Marco Para Entender La Pobreza (*Spanish translation of
    Framework)
Learning Structures
Preventing School Violence by Creating Emotional Safety. Video Series &
    Manual
Meeting Standards & Raising Test Scores – When you don't have much
    time or money Video Series & Manual (Payne & Magee)
Removing the Mask: Giftedness in Poverty (Payne & Slocumb)
Bridges Out of Poverty. Strategies for Professionals and Communities
    (Payne, Devol & Smith)
Think Rather of Zebra (Stailey & Payne)
What Every Church Member Should Know About Poverty (Payne & Ehlig)
Living on a Tightrope – a Survival Handbook for Principals (Payne &
    Sommers)
Hidden Rules of Class at Work (Payne & Krabill)

Ruby K. Payne, Ph.D.

UNDERSTANDING LEARNING
the How, the Why, the What

TABLE OF CONTENTS

INTRODUCTION

Teaching vs. Learning

Teaching is outside the head and the body; learning is inside the head and the body.

This book will look at learning – what is inside the head and the body.

Let's make a simplified analogy to a computer. The brain is the hardware; the mind is the software. Learning is about the development and use of the software. Just as  hardware and software must have each other in order to function, so the brain must have a mind. So must teaching and learning go together. But they are not the same thing. In order to teach, one must know what needs to go on inside a student's head. That's what this book is.

[For those of you familiar with brain research and cognitive studies, this book is a synopsis of those findings. Please do not be offended by this effort to offer the fruits of that research to a wider audience.]

CHAPTER ONE

The Brain and the Mind

> # It is possible to have a brain and not have a mind. A brain is inherited; a mind is developed.
>
> –Feuerstein

To begin our discussion, a distinction will be made between the brain and the mind. Truth be told, it is all one and the same. But for the purposes of this book, the brain is going to mean what you inherited and the mind will be what was developed by your environment. Cognitive scientists have concluded that it's about a 50-50 arrangement. About half of who an individual becomes is developed by his/her genetic code and about half by his/her environment.

All functions of the brain are either a chemical or electrical interaction. A chemical interaction occurs on the face of the cell and continues down the tail (axon) of the cell as an electrical impulse. When the electrical impulse enters the dendrites and synapses, causing their structure to permanently change, learning has occurred.

Therefore, learning is physiological. That's why it takes so long to "unlearn" something that has been learned incorrectly.

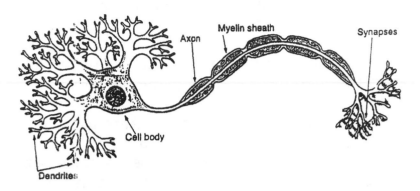

Chemicals in the brain come from four sources: what the genetic code indicates will be made, hormonal fluctuations, external experience (you get frightened and produce adrenaline), and what you eat and breathe.

This book is going to concentrate on the development of the mind. What is the mind as it's being defined here? It is the part that was learned in the environment. But more importantly, it is the abstract replication/representation of external reality. What does that mean?

As human beings, we are limited. We cannot communicate telepathically. Wouldn't it be nice if we could communicate by, say, rubbing heads? Well, we can't. So we use abstract representational systems, which illustrate common understandings, in order to communicate. Numbers, language, drawings, etc. ... all are forms of this.

For example, in the winter, "cold" is measured by a thermometer. However, the sensory reality of cold is not the same as the measured reality of cold. After the temperature gets 10 below zero, it's hard to tell the difference between 10 below zero and 40 below zero. Both are cold. The measurement system is the abstract overlay of the sensory-based reality.

How did we get this abstract structure? We got it from the interplay of language and experience in our environment. When we were young, we were mediated by the adults in our life. What they did when they mediated us was to give us the what, the why, and the how. In other words, they pointed out the stimulus (what we were to pay attention to), gave it meaning (the why), and gave us a strategy (the how).

MEDIATION

Point out the stimulus (what)	Give it meaning (why)	Provide a strategy (how)

For example, a parent says to a child:

- "Don't cross the street without looking" (what).
- "You could be killed" (why).
- "Look both ways twice before you cross the street" (how).

This mediation builds an abstract architecture inside the child's head. That architecture acts as an abstract replication of external reality, just as the blueprint acts as an abstract replication of a house.

CHAPTER TWO

Learning (Mediation): How, Why, What

The mediation of the mind happens when an individual is taught the what, the why, and the how. Just as a computer has a programmer for the software, so a student has individuals who help develop the mind.  Reuven Feuerstein studied under Jean Piaget and asked him how he accounted for individual differences. Piaget, a biologist, was more interested in accommodation and assimilation. Feuerstein believed that when a caring adult intervened using mediation, significant learning occurred.

Mediation is particularly required when an individual is a new learner to a skill, process, content ... whatever.

Research on new learners (Bloom and Berliner) indicates that there is a process that an individual goes through.

NOVICE	Has no experience with information, skill, process, etc. Needs terminology, models, and procedures. Needs context-free rules.
ADVANCED BEGINNER	Has some experience and begins to collect episodic knowledge (stories) and strategic knowledge (strategies). Begins to see similarities across contexts or situations that he/she is in.
COMPETENT	Can make conscious choices about what will and will not work. Can distinguish important from unimportant. Takes personal responsibility for his/her learning because he/she knows what he/she did to make a difference.

| PROFICIENT | Sees hundreds of patterns and sorts information quickly by pattern. Uses intuition and know-how to make judgments. Has wealth of experience from which to make generalizations and judgments. |
| EXPERT | Makes his/her own rules because of extensive experience. Performance is so fluid it can happen virtually without conscious thought; this is called automaticity. |

A beginning learner in anything needs the three components of mediation – the what, the why, and the how. Often the expert has difficulty helping a novice because so many of the expert's actions are at the level of automaticity, and the expert has a great deal of difficulty articulating what he/she is doing. This dynamic is frequently seen in sports.

There is a rule in cognitive research that goes like this:

The more complex the process an individual is involved in, the more parts of that process need to be at the level of automaticity.

For example, when a child learns to ride a bicycle, training wheels are often used. But a skilled rider would never use training wheels. What the training wheels allow the child to do is learn to steer, guide, pedal, and brake. When those are more at the level of automaticity, then the training wheels are taken off, and additional skills are developed.

So it's a mistake to teach beginners in the same way one would teach a skilled individual.

Second, the brain processes things differently when one is a new learner.

In the book *Making Connections* (1991) by Caine and Caine, the authors describe two different kinds of memory functions in the brain. One is used by beginning learners (taxon), while the other is used by individuals who have more experience with it (locale).

TAXON	LOCALE
No context (experience)	Context (experience)
Memory capacity: about five things	Unlimited memory
Requires continuous rehearsal to remember	Remembers quickly but has loss of accessibility over period of time
Is in short-term memory	Is in long-term memory
Limited to extrinsic motivation	Motivated by novelty, curiosity, expectation (intrinsic)
Specific, habit-like behaviors that are resistant to change	Updated continuously, flexible
Isolated items	Interconnected, spatial memory
Not connected to meaning	Has meaning that is motivated by need to make sense
Acquisition of relatively fixed routes	Forms initial maps quickly and involves sensory activity and emotion; generates personal maps through creation of personal meaning
Follows route	Uses map

What this means is that a beginning learner must be mediated in order to learn. He/she must be given the what, the why, and the how.

Often in schools, the focus is on the content; the why and how are seldom if ever mentioned, so the student is unable to do the work.

CHAPTER THREE

Abstract Representational Systems

One of the reasons you and I are successful is that we have been mediated, not only in sensory data, but also in abstract data. What does that mean?

Just as a computer has icons to represent the software, so does the mind.

A Dutch linguist, Martin Joos, has researched language and has found that no matter which language in the world one speaks, there are five registers.

FROZEN	Words are always the same (i.e., Lord's Prayer, Pledge of Allegiance, etc.).
FORMAL	Word choice and sentence structure of business and educational community; 1,200– to 1,600-word spoken vocabulary.
CONSULTATIVE	A mix of formal and casual register.

| CASUAL | Language between friends. Comes out of oral tradition of any country. Has few abstract words, uses non-verbal assists, and has 400- to 800-word spoken vocabulary. |
| INTIMATE | Language between lovers or twins. Private language shared between two individuals and understood by those individuals. |

The research indicates that there is a strong relationship between the amount of vocabulary an individual has and social class. In generational poverty, it is not unusual for individuals to know only casual register. An individual who has only casual register does not have many abstract words. The abstract words are in formal register.

Hart and Risley in *Meaningful Differences in the Everyday Experience of Young American Children* (1995) found the following patterns in children between the ages of 1 and 3 in stable households.

Welfare households	Child heard average of 10 million words
Working-class households	Child heard average of 20 million words
Professional households	Child heard average of 30 million words

Language or words are the tools of ideas. Abstract words represent those ideas, concepts, processes, etc., that do not have sensory-based representations.

What are these abstractions or representations?

A few summers ago it was so hot in Fort Worth, Texas, that the railroad tracks warped. We keep butter out in our house, and it kept melting. One day I said to my husband, "The thermometer says it's 72 degrees in here, but the butter is melting. In the winter, it says 72 degrees and the butter does not melt." He said, "Do not confuse real heat with measured heat."

You see, Anders Celsius and Gabriel Fahrenheit decided they wanted a better way to talk about heat, so each designed a system to do so. But the systems are abstract representations and measurements of a sensory-based reality.

VS.

Language is the tool we use to create and acknowledge those abstract systems. Abstract systems are learned. If a student comes from an environment where there is a heavy reliance on casual register, and there isn't much formal education, often the student has few abstract representational systems. <u>To survive in poverty, one must be very sensory-based and non-verbal. To survive in school, one must be very verbal and abstract</u>.

Furthermore, abstractions are stored in the mind in either visual or auditory rhythmic memory. Abstractions are kept in mental models. <u>Mental models are in the form of a story, a metaphor, an analogy – or, perhaps, a two-dimensional drawing</u>.

For example, when a house is being built, blueprints are used. The blueprints become the

abstract representational system for the final
sensory-based object, the house.

Another example: A lawyer I know got a call
from a colleague who was in court and needed
a piece of paper from his desk. She said, "Your
desk is a mess. No one could find it." And he
said to her, "Go stand in front of my desk.
Picture an overlay of the map of the United
States. That paper is somewhere around
Vermont." And she found it. He had given her
an abstract representational system.

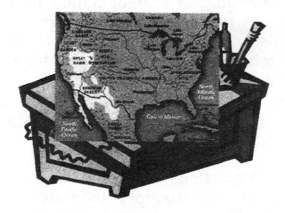

**Mental models tell either the purpose,
structure, or pattern of a subject area or
discipline.**

**To survive in the world of work or school, one
must be able to use abstract representational
systems. They are learned.**

CHAPTER FOUR

Abstract Processes (the How)

Abstract processes are "the how" and accompany all learning. Jerome Bruner says all learning is connected to the task and context of the learning. In other words, the process and the content are interwoven. To teach one without the other is to have incomplete learning.

Just as one must follow steps in software, i.e., double-click the icon, then do this ... so the mind must have procedures.

Often in schools, we do not direct-teach the process. We direct-teach the content. Reuven Feuerstein describes the abstract processes that must be used to learn.

INPUT STRATEGIES

Input is defined as "quantity and quality of the data gathered."

1. Use planning behaviors.
2. Focus perception on specific stimulus.
3. Control impulsivity.
4. Explore data systematically.
5. Use appropriate and accurate labels.

6. Organize space with stable systems of reference.
7. Orient data in time.
8. Identify constancies across variations.
9. Gather precise and accurate data.
10. Consider two sources of information at once.
11. Organize data (parts of a whole).
12. Visually transport data.

ELABORATION STRATEGIES

Elaboration is defined as "use of the data."

1. Identify and define the problem.
2. Select relevant cues.
3. Compare data.
4. Select appropriate categories of time.
5. Summarize data.
6. Project relationships of data.
7. Use logical data.
8. Test hypotheses.
9. Build inferences.
10. Make a plan using the data.
11. Use appropriate labels.
12. Use data systematically.

OUTPUT STRATEGIES

Output is defined as "communication of the data."

1. Communicate clearly the labels and process.
2. Visually transport data correctly.
3. Use precise and accurate language.
4. Control impulsive behavior.

Where does an individual get these strategies? Mediation builds them! Typically in school, we start teaching at the elaboration level, i.e., the use of the data. When students don't understand, we reteach these strategies but don't revisit the quality and quantity of the data gathered – namely, the input strategies.

In order to better understand input strategies, each is explained in more detail. Typically, input strategies are not directly taught, because we don't know how to teach them. The assumption is that everyone has them. For those students who don't have these strategies, however, the strategies can be directly taught to students.

INPUT STRATEGIES

Using planning behaviors includes goal setting, identifying the procedures in the task, identifying parts of the task, assigning time to the task(s), and identifying the quality of the work necessary to complete the task.

Focusing perception on a specific stimulus is the strategy of seeing every detail on the page or in the environment. It is the strategy of identifying everything noticed by the five senses.

Controlling impulsivity is the strategy of stopping action until one has thought about the task. There is a direct correlation between planning and impulse control.

Exploring data systematically means that a strategy is employed to procedurally and systematically go through every piece of data. Numbering is a way to go systematically through data. Highlighting important data is another way.

Using appropriate and accurate labels (vocabulary) is the precise use of words to identify and explain. If a student does not have specific words to use, then his/her ability to retrieve and use information is severely limited.

It's not enough that a student can do a task, he/she also must be able to label the procedures, tasks, and processes so that the task can be successfully repeated each time and analyzed at a metacognitive level. Metacognition is the ability to think about one's thinking. To do so, labels must be attached. Only when labels are attached can the task be evaluated and, therefore, improved.

Organizing space with stable systems of reference is crucial to success in math. It means that up, down, across, right, left, horizontal, vertical, diagonal, east, west, north, south, etc., are understood. It means that an individual can identify with words the position of an item. It means an individual can organize space. For example, he/she can find things on a desk. It means that a person can read a map. If an individual does not have this ability, then it's virtually impossible to tell a *p* from a *b* from a *d*. The only differentiation is the orientation to space.

Orienting data in time is the strategy of assigning abstract values to time and the use of the measurements of time. Without an abstract sense of time that includes a past, present, and future, a student cannot plan, he/she cannot sequence, and he/she cannot match time and task (and, therefore, doesn't get work done).

<u>Identifying constancies across variations</u> is the strategy of knowing what always remains the same and what changes. For example, if you don't know what always makes a square a square, you cannot identify constancies. This strategy enables the individual to define things, to recognize a person or an object, and to compare and contrast. This strategy also allows cursive writing to be read in all its variations.

<u>Gathering precise and accurate data</u> is the use of specific vocabulary and word choice, identifying precisely when something occurred in time and where it occurred in space, knowing the constancies, and exploring the data systematically.

<u>Considering two sources of information at once</u> means that the mind can hold two objects simultaneously and compare and contrast the two objects. To do this, the individual must be able to visually transport data accurately, identify the constancies and variations, and go through the data systematically. When those processes are completed, the student must be able to assign new vocabulary (if things have changed) and reassign existing vocabulary.

<u>Organizing data (parts of a whole)</u> involves going through data systematically, organizing space, identifying constancies and variations,

and using vocabulary to label both the parts and the whole.

<u>Visually transporting data</u> is when the eye picks up data, then carries it accurately into the brain, examines it for constancies and variations, and labels the parts and the whole. If a student cannot visually transport data, then he/she often cannot read, has difficulty with basic identification of anything, and cannot copy.

What does this mean in the classroom?

When a student cannot:	One will often see this:
Use planning behaviors …	Does not get his/her work done, is impulsive.
Focus perception on a specific stimulus …	Misses parts of the task; cannot find the information on the page.
Control impulsivity …	Cannot plan.
Explore data systematically …	Does not have a method for checking work, for getting all the work done, and for finding complete answers.

Use appropriate and accurate labels (vocabulary) ...	Does not have the words to explain; cannot label processes; uses generic words, e.g., "Get that thing."
Organize space with stable systems of reference ...	Cannot read a map; cannot use the procedures in math.
Orient data in time ...	Cannot sequence or plan; cannot follow directions.
Identify constancies across variations ...	Cannot make judgments or generalizations; cannot identify patterns.
Gather precise and accurate data ...	Cannot tell specifically when, where, and how something happened.
Consider two sources of information at once ...	Cannot compare and contrast; does a different assignment the way the first one was done, whether appropriate or not.
Organize data (parts of a whole) ...	Cannot explain why; does not recognize when something is missing.
Visually transport data ...	Cannot cheat because he/she cannot copy.

How does the teacher embed these processes and develop minds?

One way is to teach these processes with all content to all students. The way I approached it in my teaching career was to use four simple processes – sorting, question making, planning to control impulsivity, and planning and labeling tasks – because these processes embed into all content, use all the input strategies, and are quick and easy.

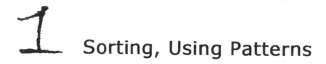 Sorting, Using Patterns

In brain research what is fairly clear is that the information must be sorted or "chunked" in order to be remembered. Details are not remembered over time, but patterns are. So if you teach patterns directly and then teach students to sort what is and is not important in relation to the patterns, the students will learn much more quickly.

In problem solving at work or school, it's very important that the worker or student is able to sort through a great deal of information quickly. He/she does this by going through patterns. For

example, if you want to buy shoes at a
department store, you don't wander aimlessly
through the store. You know that a department
store is arranged in predictable patterns. You
find the shoe department.

So for any content you're teaching, teach the
patterns and mental models of the content.
That will help students sort what is and is not
important in the learning.

2 Question Making

A quick approach is to give students the
question stems and then have them use the
rules to develop a multiple-choice question.
Developing multiple-choice questions develops
critical-thinking skills. Some examples follow.

Reading-Objective Question Stems

Objective 1: Word Meaning
In this story the word _____ means ...
The word _____ in this passage means ...

Objective 2: Supporting Ideas
What did _____ do after ...?
What happened just before _____ ...?

What did _____ do first? Last?
According to the directions given, what was
_____ supposed to do first?
After _____? Last?
Where does this story take place?
When does the story take place?

Objective 3: Summarizing Written Texts

Which sentence tells the main idea of the story?
This story is mainly about ...
What is the main idea of paragraph 3?
What is the story mostly about?
Which statement best summarizes this passage
(paragraph)?

Objective 4: Perceiving Relationships and Recognizing Outcomes

Why did __ *(name)* __ do __ *(action)* ___?
What will happen as a result of _____?
Based on the information, which is _____
most likely to do?
What will happen to _____ in this story?
You can tell from this passage that _____
is most likely to ...

Objective 5: Analyzing Information to Make Inferences and Generalizations

How did _____ feel about _____?
How does _____ feel at the beginning
(end) of the story?
According to Figure 1, what ... (or where ... how
many ... when ...) is ...?
The ___ *(event)* ___ is being held in order to ...

By ____ *(action)* ____, ____ *(name)* ____ was able to show that ...

You can tell from this passage that ...?

Which word best describes _____'s feelings in this passage?

Objective 6: Distinguishing Between Fact and Opinion

Which of these is a fact expressed in the passage?

Which of these is an opinion expressed in the passage?

Question-Making Stems
(from Texas Assessment of Academic Skills)

1. What does the word _____ mean?
2. What can you tell from the following passage?
3. What does the author give you reason to believe?
4. What is the best summary of this passage?
5. Which of the following is a <u>fact</u> in this passage?
6. What is the main idea of the _____ paragraph?
7. Which of the following is an opinion in this passage?
8. What happens after _____?
9. How did _____ feel when _____?
10. What is the main idea of this passage?
11. Which of these happened (first/last) in the passage?
12. Which of these is <u>not</u> a fact in the passage?
13. Where was _____?

14. When did _____?
15. What happens when _____?
16. What was the main reason for the following
    _____?
17. After _____, what could _____?
18. Where does the _____ take place?
19. Which of these best describes _____
    before/after _____?

Taken from Julie Ford

More Question-Making Stems

1. From this passage (story), how might
   _____ be described?
2. Why was _____?
3. Why did _____?
4. How else might the author have ended the
   passage (story)?
5. If the author had been _____, how might
   the information have been different?
6. In this passage, what does _____ mean?
7. How did _____ feel about _____?
8. What caused _____ to _____?
9. What is _____?
10. When _____ happened, why did
    _____?
11. The passage states that _____.
12. Why is that information important to
    the reader?

3 Planning to Control Impulsivity

Planning is the key to the tasks that get finished and to the control of impulsivity. Even more importantly, brain research indicates that the primary filter for what gets noticed by the mind is closely correlated with the goals of the person. So when there is no planning, there are no goals. Emotional need or association, then, determines activities.

To teach planning it's important to teach students to plan backwards. Stephen Covey, in *The Seven Habits of Highly Successful People* (1989), says, "Begin with the end in mind." In order to accomplish this "backwards planning," the teacher simply has students go to the end first, then the day or task before that, and so forth.

It's also very important in the planning process that abstract time (minutes, hours, days, weeks) gets assigned to the task.

Planning Backwards

Planning and Labeling Tasks

In addition to controlling impulsivity, planning allows a person to finish tasks. To complete tasks, both labels (vocabulary) and procedures must be used. In addition, teachers need a method for addressing each part of the task, i.e., having a systematic method for getting it all done and checking to see that it has been done.

Process (the how) is crucial to any learning; this must be taught.

In the following example, a battery is made. The left-hand column (on page 40) tells the steps that were followed. The right-hand column tells <u>why</u>. In the left-hand column ...

Step 1 The student fills a bowl with vinegar.

Step 2 The student puts pieces of cloth in the vinegar and squeezes them out.

Step 3 The student takes a piece of copper and a piece of zinc and puts the squeezed-out cloth between the copper and zinc.

Step 4 The student makes four of the items identified in Step 3.

Step 5 A piece of aluminum foil is put on the bottom of the stack of four and curved to the top of the stack.

Step 6 A small light connects the foil pieces and the stack of four. If the light goes on, the battery is completed.

HOW (Process)	WHY (Concept)
1.	Electrons, ions
2.	Insulator
3. Copper, cloth, zinc	+ −
4.	Current
5.	Circuit
6.	Closes circuit

On the right-hand side is the label, or the why ...

Step 1 Why do we need the vinegar?
  Because it provides electrons and ions.

Step 2 Why do we need the cloth dipped in vinegar? *Because it provides a conductor and insulator.*

Step 3 Why do we need the copper and zinc?
  Because they give and take electrons.

Step 4 Why do we need the stack of four?
  Because it makes a current.

Step 5 Why do we need the aluminum foil?
  Because it makes a circuit.

Step 6 Why do we need the light?
  To close the circuit.

CHAPTER FIVE

Mental Models –
Blueprints of the Subject Matter
(the Why)

1 Mental models are how the mind holds abstract information, i.e., information that has no sensory representation.

Each of us carries much abstract information around in our head every day. How do we do this? We carry it in mental models.

Just as a computer has a file manager to represent the structure of the software content, so does the human mind.

2 All subject areas or disciplines have their own blueprints or mental models.

In other words, they have their own way to structure information. For two people to communicate, there must be shared understanding.

This shared understanding comes from the study of subject matter. All occupations and all disciplines have their own mental models. To communicate about that occupation or  discipline, an understanding of those mental models (abstract blueprints) is necessary.

3 Mental models tell us what is and is not important in the discipline. They help the mind sort.

4 Mental models often explain "the why" of things working the way they do.

Mental models tell the structure, purpose, or pattern.

That's how the mind sorts what is and is not important. The mind can only remember when it can "chunk" and sort information.

 Mental models are held in the mind as stories, analogies, or two-dimensional drawings.

 Mental models "collapse" the amount of time it takes to teach something.

Mental models of a discipline
are contained within the
structure of the curriculum.

To illustrate, math is about assigning order and
value to the universe. We tend to assign order
and value in one of three ways: numbers,
space, or time. Fractions, for example, are a
part of math curricula because fractions are the
shared understanding of parts to whole of
space. Decimals are studied because decimals
tell parts to whole of *numbers*.

Lee Shulman found in his research that the
difference between a good and excellent
teacher is the depth of understanding the latter
has of the discipline.

What are examples of mental models?
Teachers have used them forever. But, too
often, educators haven't found ways to share
them with other teachers. They are the
drawings, the verbal stories, the analogies that
are given as part of instruction. As one teacher
said, "It is how I explain it."

For example, in math a square number is a square number because it physically forms a square. Nine is a square number.

When the root of a square number is discussed, it's very easy to understand. The square root of 9 is 3 because no matter how you draw the lines you will always get 3. In 30 seconds you, the reader, now understand the concept of a square number and a square root.

A mental model to help understand the pattern in the multiplication of positive and negative numbers is found in this short pictorial story.

Multiplying positive and negative numbers

+ Good guy - Bad guy	+ Coming to town - Leaving town	Get
+ + - -	+ - + -	+ - - +

So, for example, the good guys (+) are coming to town (+), which is good. Translated to math, it would read: a positive number (+) multiplied by a positive number (+) yields a positive number (+), and so on.

 There are generic mental models.

In addition to having mental models for subject areas or disciplines, there also are mental models for occupations. To be successful in work or school one must have four generic mental models. They are: space, time, part to whole, and formal register. These mental models are basic to all tasks.

Space

Space becomes important because your body operates in space. The mind must have a way to keep track of your body. One way is to touch everything. Another way is to assign a reference system to space using abstract words and drawings. For example, we talk about east, west, north, south, up, down, etc. Because math is about assigning order and value to the universe, we tend to do it directionally. Another illustration: We write small to large numbers from left to right. To read a map, one must have a reference for space. To find things in your office or desk, there must be an abstract referencing system for space.

One way to initially teach the concept of space is as follows ...

aha! Process, Inc. • (800) 424-9484

On which side of the tip of the arrow is the dot?

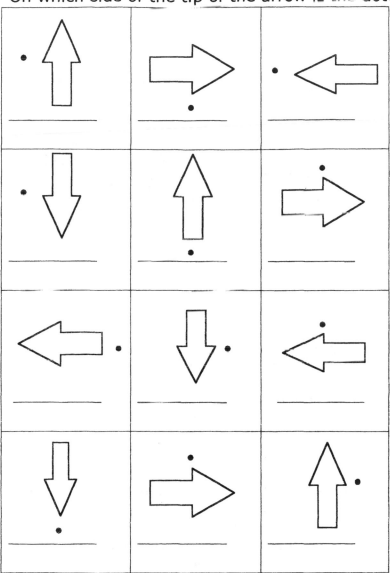

Time

A mental model for abstract time (days, minutes, weeks, hours, etc.) is crucial to success in school and work. One way to keep time is emotionally (how it feels), but another is abstractly with a calendar or a clock. Past, present, and future must be in the mental model because, without these, it isn't possible to sequence.

If you cannot sequence, then ...	You cannot plan.
If you cannot plan, then ...	You cannot predict.
If you cannot predict, then ...	You cannot identify cause and effect.
If you cannot identify cause and effect, then ...	You cannot identify consequence.
If you cannot identify consequence, then ...	You cannot control impulsivity.
If you cannot control impulsivity, then ...	You have an inclination toward criminal behavior.

Examples of a mental model for time would be a timeline, calendar, schedule, or clock.

Part to Whole

Part to whole means that one can identify the parts, as well as the whole. For example, chapters make a book. Words make a sentence. You cannot analyze anything unless you understand part to whole.

Formal Register

Because formal register is the language currency of work and school, it becomes crucial to have an understanding of it. Simple tools have been developed by Project Read. Some Project Read examples would look like this.

Sentence frame

Reminds me that a sentence must have a capital letter at the beginning and some kind of punctuation at the end.

? . !

Bare-bones sentence

Teri danced .

A sentence must contain a subject and an action.

The subject names a <u>person</u>, <u>place</u>, <u>thing</u>, or <u>idea</u>.

The action of the subject expresses <u>physical</u> or <u>mental</u> action, such as the following examples.

moved   kicked   thought   imagined

Predicate expanders

The predicate can be expanded by expressing the

how   when   where   why

of the action.

Example: **how**   **where**
The <u>waves</u> pounded relentlessly against the small boat

why   **when**
because of the violent winds during the storm.

Predicate expanders:

How	– adverbs	-ly ending, like or as, with/without
When	= time	before, during, after, when, while, since
Where	= prepositional phrases	to, from, against, behind
Why	= reason	because, to, so, for

(The opening sentence of each new paragraph should contain four expanders.)

Subject describers

Words that describe physical characteristics, personality, numbers, and ownership.

For more information on Project Read, please contact Victoria Green or Mary Lee Enfield at (800) 450-0343.

10 Sketching is a technique that can be used in the classroom to identify each student's mental models.

Simply ask students to sketch (draw in two dimensions) what a word or concept means to them. If they cannot sketch anything, it probably is not inside their head.

Examples of sketching:

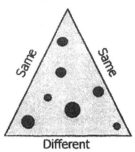

I saw an <u>isosceles</u>
triangle in my refrigerator.

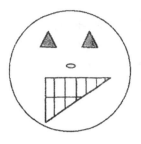

I often see a <u>scalene</u>
triangle on Kenny's face.

My friend the <u>rhombus</u> is
known as the
"Dancing Wonder."

I found four <u>vertices</u>
on a box of cereal.

Using mental models makes both teaching *and*
learning much easier.

CHAPTER SIX

Content (the What)

The content – or "the what" of learning – is the part of instruction that is usually focused on. When the processes (the how) and the blueprints of the subject matter (the why) are direct-taught, the content tends to fall into place.

Just as a computer has files, so does the mind.

Content is organized by the constructs of the disciplines (or the mental models). Here are some examples.

Content	Purpose
Language Arts	Using structure and language to communicate
Math	Assigning order and value to the universe
Biology	Identifying living systems and relationships within and among those systems
Chemistry	Bonding
Algebra	Solving for the unknown through functions
Geometry	Using logic to order and assign values to form and space
Physics	Using matter and energy through math applications

| Social Studies | Identifying patterns of people and governments over time |
| Earth Science | Identifying and predicting physical phenomena |

For example, because Language Arts is about using structure and language to communicate, virtually all Language Arts curriculum at the secondary level is divided by genres, i.e., poetry, drama, grammar, etc. Those curriculum divisions end up reflecting the structures of the various disciplines.

Why is this important?

The structure of the discipline becomes significant because it identifies what is and is not important. The research indicates that instructional time is a huge factor in learning.

So the questions in this context are: Is it cute or does it count? Does the information presented/explored promote an understanding of the constructs and use of the discipline?

When teachers or other staff persons in a building are deciding "the what" of learning (namely, the content), it's very important to address the amount of time that will be given to learning that chunk of information.

Why is this important to the learner?

If adequate time is not spent on what is important – on what counts – the learner will not have learned enough to sort what is and isn't important in that subject area. Therefore, the learner will not be able to use the information in any competent manner.

CHAPTER SEVEN

Motivation for Learning

Probably the most frequently asked question by teachers is this: How can I get my students to want to learn? Dr. James Comer says it best:

> # No significant learning occurs without a significant relationship [of mutual respect].
>
> –Comer

What does that mean? Quite simply (going back to the computer analogy), if there isn't someone at the keyboard or entering via voice, nothing happens.

And so it is with learning. It requires human interaction. At the heart of all learning are relationships.

How do you recognize relationships of mutual respect?

Generally, in relationships of mutual respect, three things are present:

Support, insistence, and high expectations

How do support, insistence, and high expectations show up in the classroom? Support becomes the direct-teaching of process and mental models; insistence is the motivation and persistence that comes from the relationship; and high expectations constitute the approach of "I know you can do it, and you will."

When there isn't mutual respect, one person becomes the taker, and the other becomes the giver. Eventually both parties come to dislike or even despise each other.

Many teachers believe that if they are nice to students, students will be nice to them. Not so. Mutual respect is taught, and mutual respect is learned.

All learning is double-coded.

In the book *The Growth of the Mind and the Endangered Origins of Intelligence* (1997), Stanley Greenspan and Beryl Benderly say all learning is double-coded, both mentally and emotionally.

It's very important to understand the emotional underpinnings of learning. All learning is in essence emotional, and virtually all learning starts with significant relationships.

The primary motivator for the development of each stage is a significant relationship.

Six developmental stages in the learning process occur when relationships are supportive and nurturing.

These six stages are:

STAGE	EXPLANATION
1. Ability to attend	To pay attention to the sensory data in the environment. The earliest sensory data – touch, taste, sound, smell, sight – result from the interplay of relationships.

2. Ability to engage	To experience feelings – joy, pleasure, anger, emotional warmth, disappointment, assertiveness, etc. Intimacy and relating begin at this stage.
3. Ability to be intentional	To create and direct desire. To use non-verbals with purpose and intention. For example, I (as an infant) want you to hold me, so I hold up my arms, and you pick me up.
4. Ability to form complex interactive patterns	To connect and use one's own intentional signals in interaction with another to negotiate and to receive security, acceptance, and approval.
5. Ability to create images, symbols, and ideas	To give abstract mental constructs emotional meaning and significance. This is the basis of reasoning and emotion-based coping strategies. When images, symbols, and ideas don't have emotional investment, they are fragmented.

6. Ability to connect images, symbols, and ideas	To develop the infrastructure and architecture of the mind. To "image" one's own feelings and desires and to understand emotional signals from others.

In discussing the six stages, one overriding reality must be remembered:

Emotion organizes experience and behavior.

STAGE ONE: Ability to Attend

At the very beginning of learning, the infant must sort out what the sensations are and what they mean. Those earliest sensations almost always come through relationships. Someone is holding the child. Someone is feeding the child. The child must stay calm enough to notice the sensations he/she is experiencing. The child must find patterns in the sensations. From these patterns come security and order. From this security and order comes the ability to regulate the mind.

STAGE TWO: Ability to Engage

When young children can attend to the surroundings and actions of the people who are their caretakers, they become engaged. The caretaker smiles, and they smile. In short, the child mirrors the expressions of the caretaker.

Greenspan and Benderly say it well:

> Without some degree of this ecstatic wooing by at least one adult who adores her, a child may never know the powerful intoxication of human closeness, never abandon herself to the magnetic pull of human relationships ... Whether because her nervous system is unable to sustain the sensations of early love or her caregiver is unable to convey them, such a child is at risk of becoming self-absorbed or an unfeeling, self-centered, aggressive individual who can inflict injury without qualm or remorse (p. 51).

STAGE THREE: Ability to Be Intentional

At this preverbal stage, a purposeful exchange of signals and responses is used to elicit what the child desires. In this stage the child learns to distinguish between you and me, i.e., from self and other. Boundaries are established. When responses are inappropriate, the child becomes disorganized and eventually loses interest. For example, if a person is talking to someone with a "poker face," eventually the conversation becomes fragmented; the speaker loses interest and gives up.

Interactions become purposeful, and "willful reciprocity" occurs, which also signals a higher developmental level of the central nervous system.

Desires or wishes are tied to actions, not ideas. Desires or wishes also are linked to subjective needs, not objective needs.

STAGE FOUR: Ability to Form Complex Interactive Patterns

At this stage, purpose and interaction become the focus. The child learns to communicate across space, i.e., I am not touching my caregiver. She is in the next room, but I know she is there. This gives a strong sense of emotional security. Imitation is a part of this stage. The child mimics what the adult does. At this stage, a child's emotions are attached to patterns of response. Attitudes and values start here. Meaning is established from patterns of desire, expectation, and intention.

STAGE FIVE: Ability to Create Images, Symbols, and Ideas

Here the child experiences himself/herself in images – and not just in feelings, physical sensations, and behavior. It's important to note that children who haven't mastered the previous stages tend to operate in a concrete, rote manner. At this point in time, individuals can try out behaviors and actions inside their head without actually doing them.

STAGE SIX: Ability to Connect Images, Symbols, and Ideas

At this stage, the individual connects the images, symbols and ideas that were developed in Stage Five to an architecture in which abstractions are emotionally embedded and interwoven. The individual is able to view emotions abstractly and work through them both at a feeling level and a cognitive one. Sorting occurs both cognitively and through emotion.

Learning the Abstract

Because schools and the work setting operate at stages five and six, many individuals are new learners to the abstract. There is a process that a person goes through when he/she is learning something new. That process was discussed in Chapter Two.

How does a student know that a teacher has respect for him/her?

Two pieces of research are particularly instructive. One is from Stephen Covey, and the other is research by TESA (Teacher Expectations and Student Achievement).

Covey states that relationships of mutual respect are like bank accounts. You make emotional deposits to those relationships, and you make emotional withdrawals from the relationships. When the withdrawals are substantially greater than the deposits, the relationship is soon broken.

DEPOSITS	WITHDRAWALS
Seek first to understand	Seek first to be understood
Keeping promises	Breaking promises
Kindnesses, courtesies	Unkindnesses, discourtesies
Clarifying expectations	Violating expectations
Loyalty to the absent	Disloyalty, duplicity
Apologies	Pride, conceit, arrogance
Open to feedback	Rejecting feedback

Chart adapted from The Seven Habits of Highly Effective People *(1989) by* Stephen Covey

The TESA research describes 15 behaviors that teachers use with students when there is mutual respect between teacher and student. The study found that when these behaviors are used with all students, learning jumps dramatically.

Here are the 15 behaviors of mutual respect:

1.	Calls on everyone in the room equitably.
2.	Provides individual help.
3.	Gives "wait time" (allows student enough time to answer).
4.	Asks questions to give the student clues about the answer.
5.	Asks questions that require more thought.
6.	Tells students whether their answers are right or wrong.
7.	Gives specific praise.
8.	Gives reasons for praise.
9.	Listens.
10.	Accepts the feelings of the student.
11.	Gets within an arm's reach of each student each day.
12.	Is courteous to students.
13.	Shows personal interest and gives compliments.
14.	Touches students (appropriately).
15.	Desists (does not call attention to every misbehavior).

TESA copyright is held by Los Angeles Board of Education.

When we asked students in our research how
they knew the teacher had respect for them,
repeatedly we heard the following:

- The teacher calls me by my name, not
  "Hey you."
- The teacher answers my questions.
- The teacher cares about me.
- The teacher talks to me respectfully.
- The teacher notices me and says hi.
- The teacher helps me when I need help.

What does this mean in practice?

If a student and teacher don't
have a relationship of mutual
respect, the learning will be
significantly reduced and, for
some students, it won't occur
at all.

If a student and teacher don't
like each other – or even come
to despise each other – forget
about significant positive
learning. If mutual respect is
present, that can compensate
for the dislike.

CHAPTER EIGHT

Difficult Students, Difficult Classrooms

These questions inevitably come up:

What do I do when more than 40% of the students are difficult? How can learning take place with so many difficult students?

What do I do with a student who habitually breaks relationships with adults?

What do I do with the student who has biochemical issues? Has neurological damage?

To use our analogy to the computer, what do I do when the computer freezes? When the hard drive crashes? When the software doesn't do what it's supposed to?

As you know, just like the computer, not everything can be "fixed." But what we do know are ways to minimize the interruptions and address the learning.

Some suggestions:

1. <u>Always direct-teach the mental models of the content you are teaching</u>. Fewer

discipline problems occur when students are learning.

2. <u>Direct-teach the processes and procedures you want to occur in your classroom</u>. Have students practice those. Remember that 95% of discipline problems in classrooms occur the first five and last five minutes of class. Harry Wong, in his book *The First Day of School* (1998), has a number of excellent suggestions.

3. <u>Build relationships of mutual respect with the "troublemakers."</u> Ninety percent of discipline problems come from 5% of the students. Humor (not sarcasm) is one of the best tools for developing mutual respect; students particularly look to see if you have a sense of humor about yourself. Furthermore, students won't respect you unless you are personally strong. So if you show fear, you won't be respected.

4. <u>Tightly structure tasks by time and procedure</u>. Do so by giving students the steps – in writing – necessary to do the task, noting specific time frames in which to do it. Then have students work in pairs

where they talk to each other while doing the task. More learning usually occurs collaboratively than alone. Typically students are going to talk anyway, so have them talk about their learning. The pair stays together for the duration of that task. And if for some reason the student doesn't like you, he/she may like the person with whom he/she is working.

5. <u>Use a choice/consequence approach to discipline</u>. In other words, if a student "messes up" after having heard clear expectations of appropriate behavior, simply express your regret that he/she made a poor choice – and quickly and matter-of-factly establish a natural consequence for the student's misstep.

6. <u>Have students do a simple planning/goal-setting task each day around their work</u>. It will significantly lessen impulsivity.

7. <u>Use a contract system to address individual needs, as well as address different times of finishing work</u>. I did this with ninth-graders. One day a week the students worked independently; it was 20% of their grade. At the beginning of each grading period, I gave them a list of

activities they could choose from. Each activity had points assigned to it, and the student was to identify 100 points toward which he/she would work. The students divided the activities by week and identified what they would finish each week. If a student was particularly weak in a certain area, I would tell him/her to get some points from that area. If a student finished early, I would say, "Go work on your contract." That way students were always busy and always learning.

8. Separate students who must be separated. Talk to your administrator about any student combinations that are problematic together and arrange to have them placed in different classrooms.

CONCLUSION

Learning involves both the physical (the brain) and the environmental influences (the mind). For students who haven't had much exposure to the abstract or to representational systems, they are new learners to the abstract. As new learners, they need three things: the how, the why, and the what. Then they can begin patterning information in order to use it in the long term. Since patterns seem to be related to the structure of the subject matter, it's important to teach mental models.

Because virtually all learning involves emotion, relationships of mutual respect energize, at the most basic level, the motivation to learn.

To close with our computer analogy, the hardware (the brain) needs the software (the mind) to function. Nothing functions without the person at the keyboard or the individual giving voice commands – just as next to nothing in learning occurs without relationships of mutual respect.

BIBLIOGRAPHY

Allee, Verna. (1997). *The Knowledge Evolution: Building Organizational Intelligence.* Newton, MA: Butterworth-Heinnemann.

Anderson, John R. (1996). *The Architecture of Cognition.* Mahwah, NJ: Lawrence Erlbaum Associates, Publishers.

Berliner, D.C. (1988). Implications of studies of expertise in pedagogy for teacher education and evaluation. Paper presented at Educational Testing Service Invitational Conference on New Directions for Teacher Assessment, New York, NY.

Biemiller, Andrew. (2000). Vocabulary: the missing link between phonics and comprehension. *Perspectives,* Fall, 26-30.

Bloom, Benjamin. (1976). *Human Characteristics and School Learning.* New York, NY: McGraw-Hill Book Company.

Brandt, Ron. (1988). On assessment of teaching: a conversation with Lee Shulman. *Educational Leadership,* November, 42-46.

Bransford, John D., Brown, Ann L., & Cocking, Rodney R. (Eds.). (1999). *How People Learn: Brain, Mind, Experience and School.* Washington, DC: National Academy Press.

Caine, Renate Nummela, & Caine, Geoffrey. (1991). *Making Connections: Teaching and the Human Brain.* Alexandria, VA: Association for Supervision and Curriculum Development, Publishers.

Caine, Renate Nummela, & Caine, Geoffrey. (1997). *Education on the Edge of Possibility.* Alexandria, VA: Association for Supervision and Curriculum Development.

Coles, Robert. (1989). *The Call of Stories: Teaching and the Moral Imagination.* Boston, MA: Houghton Mifflin Company.

Costa, Arthur, & Garmston, Robert. (1986). *The Art of Cognitive Coaching: Supervision for Intelligent Teaching.* Sacramento, CA: California State University Press.

Covey, Stephen R. (1989). *The Seven Habits of Highly Effective People: Powerful Lessons in Personal Change.* New York, NY: Simon & Schuster.

Crowell, Sam. (1989). A new way of thinking: the challenge of the future. *Educational Leadership.* September, 60-64.

Damasio, Antonio R. (1994). *Descartes' Error: Emotion, Reason, and the Human Brain.* New York, NY: G.P. Putnam Sons.

DeSoto, Hernandon. (2000). *The Mystery of Capital.* New York, NY: Basic Books.

Edvinsson, Leif, & Malone, Michael S. (1997). *Intellectual Capital: Realizing Your Company's True Value by Finding Its Hidden Brainpower.* New York, NY: HarperCollins Publishers.

Egan, Kieran. (1989). Memory, imagination, and learning: connected by story. *Phi Delta Kappan,* February, 455-59.

Egan, Kieran. (1986). *Teaching as Story Telling.* Chicago, IL: University of Chicago Press.

Fassler, David G., & Dumas, Lynne S. (1997). *Help Me, I'm Sad.* New York, NY: Penguin Books.

Feuerstein, Reuven, et al. (1980). *Instrumental Enrichment: An Intervention Program for Cognitive Modifiability.* Glenview, IL: Scott, Foresman & Co.

Freire, Paulo. (2000). *Pedagogy of the Oppressed* (30th Anniversary Edition). New York, NY: Continuum International Publishing Group.

Gladwell, Malcolm. (2000). *The Tipping Point: How Little Things Make a Big Difference.* New York, NY: Little, Brown & Company.

Glickman, Carl D. (1990). *Supervision of Instruction: A Developmental Approach* (2nd Edition). Boston, MA: Allyn & Bacon.

Goleman, Daniel. (1995). *Emotional Intelligence.* New York, NY: Bantam Books.

Good, Thomas L., & Brophy, Jere E. (1991). *Looking in Classrooms* (5th Edition). New York, NY: HarperCollins Publishers.

Greenspan, Stanley I., & Benderly, Beryl L. (1997). *The Growth of the Mind and the Endangered Origins of Intelligence.* Reading, MA: Perseus Books.

Harrison, Lawrence E., & Huntington, Samuel P. (Eds.). (2000). *Culture Matters: How Values Shape Human Progress.* New York, NY: Basic Books.

Hart, Betty, & Risley, Todd R. (1995). *Meaningful Differences in the Everyday Experience of Young American Children.* Baltimore, MD: Paul H. Brookes Publishing Co.

Hock, Dee. (1999). *Birth of the Chaordic Age.* San Francisco, CA: Berrett-Koehler Publishers.

Howard, Pierce J. (2000). *The Owner's Manual for the Brain* (2nd Edition). Austin, TX: Bard Press.

Hunter, Madeline. (1982). *Mastery Teaching.* El Segundo, CA: TIP Publications.

Idol, Lorna, & Jones, B.F. (Eds.). (1991). *Educational Values and Cognitive Instruction: Implications for Reform.* Mahwah, NJ: Lawrence Erlbaum Associates, Publishers.

Jensen, Eric. (1994). *The Learning Brain.* Del Mar, CA: Turning Point Publishing.

Jones, B.F., Pierce, J., & Hunter, B. (1988). Teaching Students to construct graphic representations. *Educational Leadership,* 46 (4), 20-25.

Jordan, Heather, Mendro, Robert, & Weerasinghe, Dash. (1997). Teacher effects on longitudinal student achievement. Dallas (Texas) Public Schools. Table 3. www.edtrust.org.

Joyce, Bruce, & Showers, Beverly. (1988). *Student Achievement Through Staff Development.* New York, NY: Longman.

Joyce, Bruce, & Weil, Marsha. (1986). *Models of Teaching* (3rd Edition). Boston, MA: Allyn & Bacon.

Marzano, Robert J., & Arredondo, Daisy. (1986). *Tactics for Thinking.* Aurora, CO: Mid Continent Regional Educational Laboratory.

McCarthy, Bernice. (1996). *About Learning.* Barrington, IL: Excel.

McTighe, Jay, & Lyman, Frank T. Jr. (1988). Cueing thinking in the classroom: the promise of theory-embedded tools. *Educational Leadership,* April, 18-24.

O'Dell, Carla, & Grayson, Jackson C. Jr., with Essaides, Nilly. (1998). *If Only We Knew What We Know.* New York, NY: Free Press.

Oshry, Barry. (1995). *Seeing Systems: Unlocking the Mysteries of Organizational Life.* San Francisco, CA: Berrett-Koehler Publishers.

Palinscar, Anne S., & Brown, A.L. (1984). The reciprocal teaching of comprehension-fostering and comprehension-monitoring activities. *Cognition and Instruction,* 1 (2), 117-175.

Porter, Andrew C., & Brophy, Jere. (1988). Synthesis of research on good teaching: insights from the work of the Institute for Research on Teaching. *Educational Leadership,* May, 74-85.

Resnick, Lauren B., & Klopfer, Leopold. (Eds.). (1989). *Toward the Thinking Curriculum: Current Cognitive Research.* Alexandria, VA: Association for Supervision and Curriculum Development, Publishers.

Ridley, Matt. (2000). *Genome: The Autobiography of a Species in 23 Chapters.* New York, NY: HarperCollins Publishers.

Rieber, Robert W. (Ed.). (1997). *The Collected Works of L.S. Vygotsky (Volume 4: The History of the Development of Higher Mental Functions).* New York, NY: Plenum Press.

Rosenholtz, Susan J. (1989). *Teachers' Workplace: The Social Organization of Schools.* New York, NY: Longman.

Sander, William L., & Rivers, Joan C. (1996). Cumulative and residual effects of teachers on future student academic achievement. www.edtrust.org.

Sapolsky, Robert M. (1998). *Why Zebras Don't Get Ulcers.* New York, NY: W.H. Freeman & Co.

Senge, Peter, et al. (2000). *Schools That Learn: A Fifth Discipline Fieldbook for Educators, Parents, and Everyone Who Cares About Education.* New York, NY: Doubleday-Currency.

Senge, Peter, Ross, Richard, Smith, Bryan, Roberts, Charlotte, & Kleiner, Art. (1994). *The Fifth Discipline Fieldbook: Strategies and Tools for Building a Learning Organization.* New York, NY: Doubleday-Currency.

Sharron, Howard, & Coulter, Martha. (1996). *Changing Children's Minds: Feuerstein's Revolution in the Teaching of Intelligence* (3rd Edition). Birmingham, England: Imaginative Minds.

Shulman, Lee. (1988). A union of insufficiencies: strategies for teacher assessment in a period of educational reform. *Educational Leadership,* November, 36-41.

Shulman, Lee. (1987). Assessment for teaching: an initiative for the profession. *Phi Delta Kappan,* September, 38-44.

Stewart, Thomas A. (1997). *Intellectual Capital: The New Wealth of Organizations.* New York, NY: Doubleday-Currency.

Sveiby, Karl Erik. (1997). *The New Organizational Wealth: Managing and Measuring Knowledge-Based Assets.* San Francisco, CA: Berrett-Koehler Publishers.

Walberg, Herbert J. (1990). Productive teaching and instruction: assessing the knowledge base. *Phi Delta Kappan,* February, 470-478.

Watson, Bruce, & Knoicek, Richard. (1990). Teaching for conceptual change: confronting children's experience. *Phi Delta Kappan,* May, 680-685.

Wiggins, Grant, & McTighe, Jay. (1998). *Understanding by Design.* Alexandria, VA: Association for Supervision and Curriculum Development, Publishers.

Wilson, Edward O. (1998). *Consilience: The Unity of Knowledge.* New York, NY: Alfred A. Knopf.

Wise, Anna. (1995). *The High Performance Mind: Mastering Brainwaves for Insight, Healing, and Creativity.* New York, NY: Tarcher/Putnam.

Wong, Harry K., & Wong, Rosemary Tripi. (1998). *The First Day of School: How to Be An Effective Teacher* (Revised Edition). Mountainview, CA: Harry K. Wong, Publisher.

www.edtrust.org. (2001). *Achievement in America 2000.*

More eye-openers at ...
www.ahaprocess.com

- **Join our aha! News List!**

  Receive the latest income and poverty statistics *free* when you join! Then receive periodic news and updates, recent articles by Dr. Payne and more!

- **Register for Dr. Payne's U. S. National Tour**

- **Visit our on-line store**

  Books

  Videos

  Workshops

- **Learn about our Certified Trainer Programs**

  A Framework for Understanding Poverty

  Bridges Out of Poverty

  Meeting Standards & Raising Test Scores

- **Register for courses at our Training Center**

aha! Process, Inc.
P.O. Box 727
Highlands, TX 77562-0727
(800) 424-9484; (281) 426-5300
fax: (281) 426-5600

Want your own copy? Would you like to give a copy to a friend?

Please send me:

_____ Copy/copies of *Understanding Learning: the
How, the Why, the What*

Books: 1-4 books $10/each + $4.50 on first book, plus $2.00
                    each additional book for shipping/handling
       5 or more $7/each + 8% shipping/handling

Mail to:

Name: _____
Organization: _____
Address: _____
_____
Phone: _____ E-mail: _____
Would you like to be on aha's opt-in Email Newslist? _____

Method of payment:
PO # _____
Credit card type: _____ Exp: _____
Credit card number: _____
Check: $ _____ Check # _____

Subtotal: $ _____
Shipping: $ _____
Sales tax: $ _____ (8.25% in Texas)
Total: $_____

Or order from our on-line store at www.ahaprocess.com